3

Joan Kang Shin
JoAnn (Jodi) Crandall

SECOND EDITION • GRAMMAR WORKBOOK

**NATIONAL
GEOGRAPHIC**
L E A R N I N G

Australia · Brazil · Mexico · Singapore · United Kingdom · United States

Unit 1

before and **after**

Question						Answer
What	does	she	do	**before**	school?	She feeds her fish.
	do	you		**after**	breakfast?	I brush my teeth.

Time phrases (with *before* and *after*) in a sentence show the order of two events.

1 **Look.** Write *before* or *after*.

Before dinner	After dinner

1. The children read _____ dinner.

2. The boy combs his cat _____ dinner.

3. The boy does his homework _____ dinner.

4. He takes a shower _____ dinner.

5. The baby and the boy play _____ dinner.

6. The boy feeds his dog _____ dinner.

2 Write. Unscramble the questions about Marta's day.

1. Marta / do / school / does / after / what

   <u>What does Marta do after school</u>_____?

2. does / before / what / Marta / dinner / do

   _____?

3. dinner / she / do / does / what / after

   _____?

4. before / what / does / bedtime / do / she

   _____?

3 Read and write. Look at Marta's schedule. Answer the questions from Activity 2. Use *before* and *after*.

4.00: school ends
4.30: take dog to the park
6.00: do homework
7.00: eat dinner
8.30: feed dog
8.45: brush teeth
9.00: bedtime

1. <u>She takes her dog to the park after school.</u>

2. _____.

3. _____.

4. _____.

4 Write. What do you do? Use *before* or *after*.

1. _____ dinner.

2. _____ school.

3. _____ dinner.

4. _____ bedtime.

3

Adverbs of frequency

Omar	**always**	gets up	early.	
He	**usually**	eats	breakfast	at 6:00.
	sometimes			at 6:30.
He	**never**	makes	his bed.	

Use words like *always* and *sometimes* to describe how often you do an action.

 Read. Write the word that is true for you.

> always   never   sometimes   usually

1. I _____ eat breakfast before school.

2. I _____ help with dinner.

3. I _____ play soccer after school.

4. I _____ get up at five o'clock in the morning.

5. I _____ read before bed.

6. I _____ play with my friends after school.

7. I _____ make my bed in the morning.

8. I _____ take a shower before I go to bed.

 **Look and write.**

	M	T	W	T	F
Tamara / Ride bike	✓	✓	✓	✓	✓
Kiko / Take dog to park		✓	✓		
Olga / Do homework before school					
Marco / Help at home	✓	✓	✓		✓

Tamara _____ .

Kiko _____ .

Olga _____ .

Marco _____ .

3 **Read and write.** Answer the questions.

1. Who always makes breakfast at home?

    _____ .

2. Who sometimes helps you with your homework?

    _____ .

3. Who usually gets up before you?

    _____ .

 Write. Tell what you do on weekends. Use *always, never, sometimes,* and *usually.*

I never get up before seven o'clock on Saturday. _____

_____

_____

_____

Unit 2

Can for requests and offers

		Can	you	help	me?
Sure.	How	can	I	help?	

		on	Main Street.	
Where's the museum?	It's	next to	the police station.	where's = where is
		across from	the bakery.	
		on the corner of	Main Street and First Street.	it's = it is
		behind	the movie theater.	
		between	the park and the school.	

Use *can* to ask for and to offer help.

1 **Read and draw.** Label your drawings.

1. The museum is across from the hospital.

2. The park is behind the house.

3. The bakery is next to the restaurant.

2 **Write.** Unscramble the questions. Add punctuation marks.

1. help / you / please / can / me

_____

2. I / can / sure / how / help

_____

3. library / where / is / the

6 _____

3 **Look at the map.** Complete the sentences.

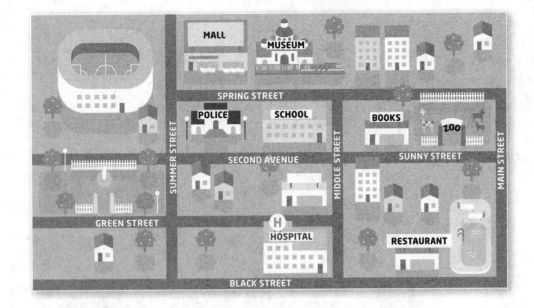

1. The school is _____ Spring Street and Second Avenue.

2. The museum is _____ the school.

3. The hospital is _____ Middle Street and Black Street.

4. The school is _____ the police station.

4 **Look and write.** Complete the dialogues. Use the map from Activity 3.

1. _____ you _____ me, please?

   _____. _____ can I help?

   _____ the school?

   It's _____.

2. _____ you _____, please?

   Sure. _____?

   _____ the police station?

   It's on the corner of _____.

Giving directions

Question	Answer			
How can I get to the post office?	**Go**	**straight**. (↑)		
	Turn	**right** (↱)	on	White Street.
		left (↰)	at	the supermarket.

Use the base form of verbs like *go* and *turn* to give directions.

1 **Look and** (circle).

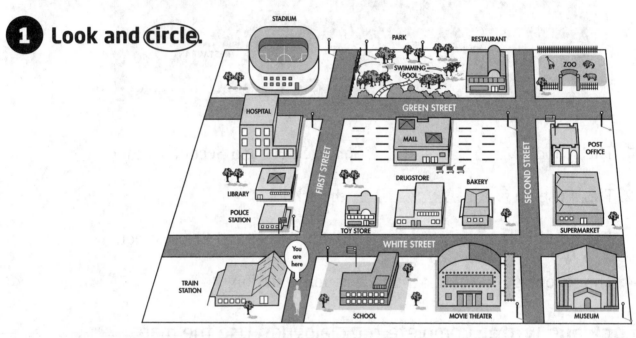

1. **How can I get to / Can you help me** the police station?

   Go straight on / Turn left on First Street.

   The police station is **across from / on the corner of** the toy store.

2. **How can I get to / Can you help me,** please?

   Yes, sure.

   How can I get to / How can I help the drugstore?

   Turn **left / right** on White Street. It's **between / across from** the toy store and the bakery.

3. **How's / How can I get to** the stadium?

   Turn left on / Go straight on First Street.

   Turn left on Green Street. / Turn right on Second Street.

   It's across from the **post office / hospital**.

2 **Look and write.** Use the map in Activity 1.

1. How can _____ the zoo?

   _____ on First Street. _____ on Green

   Street. It's _____ the post office.

2. _____ to the supermarket?

   _____ on White Street. It's _____

   Second Street and White Street.

3. _____ the hospital?

   _____ on First Street. _____ on Green Street.

   It's _____ the stadium.

3 **Look again at the map in Activity 1.** Write directions.

1. How can I get to the restaurant?

   _____

   _____

2. How can I get to the mall?

   _____

   _____

4 **Write.** Give directions from your school to your house.

   _____

   _____

   _____

Unit 3

Too for agreeing

Statement				Agreeing			Not agreeing			don't = do not
I	ride	my bike	to school.	I	**do**,	**too**.	I	**don't**.	I walk.	
Eva	takes	the bus		Her friend	**does**,	**too**.	Her friend	**doesn't**.	She drives.	doesn't = does not

Use the pattern subject + *do/does* + *too* when you agree with a statement.

 1 Read and write. Replace the underlined words.

1. I <u>do not</u> ride a scooter.   I _____ ride a scooter.

2. My brother <u>does not</u> like airplanes.   He _____ like airplanes.

3. My mom <u>does not</u> drive a car.   She _____ drive a car.

4. My friends <u>do not</u> ride their bikes to school.   They _____ ride their bikes to school.

 2 Write. Give true information.

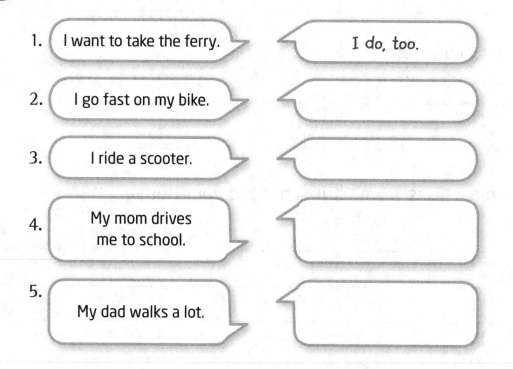

1. I want to take the ferry.   I do, too.

2. I go fast on my bike.

3. I ride a scooter.

4. My mom drives me to school.

5. My dad walks a lot.

Look and write. Complete the sentences.

Place	Scooter	Subway	Taxi	Bike
Museum		Paula	George/me	
Park	George			Paula/me
Grandparents' house	me	Paula/George		
Mall		me	George	Paula

1. I take a taxi to the museum.

George _____ *does, too* _____.
Paula _____ *doesn't* _____.
She _____ *takes the subway* _____.

2. Paula rides her bike to the park.

I _____.
George _____.
He _____.

3. George takes the subway to his grandparents' house.

Paula _____.
I _____.
I _____.

4. I take the subway to the mall.

Paula _____.
She _____.
George _____.
He _____.

4 **Write.** Think of a friend. Write three things you both do. Write two things you do differently.

I play soccer. José does, too. José plays baseball. I don't.

_____

_____

_____

_____

11

But as a contrast

| My sister takes a taxi to the mall, | **but** | my brother rides his bike. |

Use *but* to show contrast between two ideas in a sentence.

1 **Read.** Circle *and* or *but*.

1. Maya wants to go in a helicopter, **and** / **but** Dave does, too.
2. I don't take the subway very often, **and** / **but** my mom takes it every day.
3. I want to stay on the bus, **and** / **but** the driver says we must get off.
4. I go downhill fast, **and** / **but** Robert does, too.
5. My brother has a motorcycle, **and** / **but** I have a scooter.

2 **Read.** Write *but* when necessary. If *but* is not necessary, put an *X*.

1. We like reading, _____ they like watching TV.

2. I have a red scooter, _____ and Jon has one, too.

3. Giraffes have long necks _____ and long legs.

4. I can walk to the zoo, _____ Jaime can't. He takes the subway.

5. The train is fast, _____ the bus is slow.

3 **Write.** Tell what's different.

1. A motorcycle is big, <u>but a scooter is small</u>_____. (a scooter)

2. My scooter has two wheels, _____. (our car)

3. My dad takes the subway, _____. (mom / bus)

4. Sandra rides her bike at the park, _____. (walk my dog)

5. A ferry goes on water, _____. (a helicopter)

4 **Look and write.** Complete the sentences with *but*.

Me	My friend

1. I walk, _____.

2. I play baseball, _____.

3. I have a turtle, _____.

4. I eat yogurt, _____.

5 **Write.** Write four sentences about friends and family. Use the words in the box and *but*.

be	eat	go	have	like	want	wear

I am young, but my grandfather is old.

_____

_____

Units 1–3: Review

1 **Read.** Complete the conversation with words from the box.

> across from   after   always   but   do
>
> never   on the corner   sometimes   too   where's

BETTY: Hi, Laura. Do you want to go to the island this weekend? We can get the ferry with my parents. I like the ferry.

LAURA: Oh, I _____, too! What a great idea! I _____ take the ferry. My parents always drive.

BETTY: We _____ take the ferry. My parents don't like driving.

LAURA: OK. Are we going in the morning or _____ lunch?

BETTY: In the morning. Let's meet at the ferry station. Is that OK?

LAURA: Sure. _____ the ferry station?

BETTY: It's _____ of Bell Street and Anchor Road.

LAURA: Oh, yes, _____ the park. I _____ take my little brother to that park. He really likes it, _____ I think it's boring.

BETTY: I do, _____. I don't like playing there at all.

2 **Look.** Write about Karim's habits.

	M	T	W	T	F
Ride scooter	✓		✓		✓
Do homework	✓	✓	✓	✓	
Play basketball					

1. sometimes _____.

2. never _____.

3. usually _____.

3 **Look at the map.** Complete the directions.

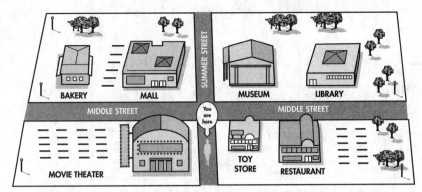

Can you help me, please?

Sure. _____?

How can I get to the library?

_____ on Summer Street. _____ on Middle Street.

It's _____ the restaurant.

4 **Look again at the map in Activity 3.** Write a dialogue. Ask for directions to the bakery.

_____

_____

_____

_____

_____

5 **Write.** Use complete sentences to write about yourself.

1. always <u>I always visit my grandma on Saturday</u> _____.

2. but _____.

3. never _____.

4. do, too _____.

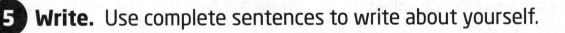

15

Unit 4

Sense verbs

The pizza	**smells**	great.	The helicopter	**sounds**	loud.
The dress	**looks**	beautiful.	The cat	**feels**	soft.

Question				Answer		
How	does	the apple	**taste**?	It	**tastes**	delicious.
	do	the rabbits	**feel**?	They	**feel**	soft.

Words like *smell, look, sound,* and *feel* are not usually used in the progressive: ~~The soup is tasting delicious.~~

 1 **Read and draw.** Draw an object for each sentence.

1. It tastes delicious.	2. It smells terrible.	3. It sounds loud.

2 **Read.** Answer the questions.

1. How does a motorcycle sound?   It <u>sounds loud</u>_____.

2. How does a rabbit feel?   It _____.

3. How does a banana taste?   It _____.

4. How does a bakery smell?   It _____.

5. How does a colorful dress look?   It _____.

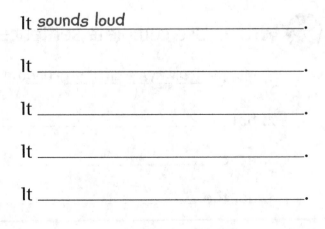

3 **Look and write.**

1.
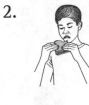
How does the trash smell? _____

It smells terrible. _____

2.

_____

_____

3.
_____

_____

4.
_____

_____

4 **Write.** Use words from each column.

airplanes		beautiful
coffee	feel	delicious
cookies	look	hard
my bed	sound	loud
paintings	taste	soft
a rock		terrible

1. A rock feels hard _____.

2. _____.

3. _____.

4. _____.

5. _____.

6. _____.

was/were

Question	Answer	Question			Answer			it's = it is
How is the bread?	It's good.	How	**was**	the bread?	It	**was**	good.	it's = it is they're = they are
How are the grapes?	They're good.	How	**were**	the grapes?	They	**were**	good.	

There are two forms for the past tense of the verb *be*: *was* and *were*

 Read and match. Draw a line.

1. How is your new bed?   a. They were salty.
2. How was the tomato soup?   b. It was hot.
3. How are your brothers?   c. It's soft.
4. How is the swimming pool?   d. They're great!
5. How were the beans?   e. It's big.

2 **Read and write.** Use the words in the box.

hard	sweet	terrible	well

1. How is your grandma?   She _____ very _____, thank you.

2. How are the new chairs? They _____ very _____.

3. How were the cookies?   They _____ _____.

4. How was the movie?   It _____ _____!

3 **Write.** Use words from the box or your own.

> delicious   easy   fun   terrible   well

1. How was your breakfast this morning? _____.

2. How is your best friend? _____.

3. How was your homework? _____.

4. How are your classes? _____.

4 **Look and write.** Use the correct tense.

> ~~bitter~~   salty   sour   spicy   sweet

1. (before) How was the tea? _____

   It was bitter! _____

2. (now) _____

   _____

3. (before) _____

   _____

4. (now) _____

   _____

5. (before) _____

   _____

Unit 5

 Read and write.

1. _____ does a hippo like mud? _____ it wants to keep cool.

2. _____ is a giraffe's neck so long? _____ the giraffe eats leaves from tall trees.

3. _____ can't penguins fly? _____ their wings are better for swimming.

4. _____ don't horses have stripes like zebras? _____ they don't have to hide in the grass.

2 **Read and write.** Write *why* or *because* and words from the box.

> bats   caves   scared

ANA: Let's explore this cave, Carlos.

CARLOS: No, thanks. I don't like caves.

ANA: _____ don't you like _____?

CARLOS: _____ _____ live in caves.

ANA: _____ don't you like bats?

CARLOS: _____ I'm _____ of them.

3 Write questions.

1. a giraffe / be tall <u>Why is a giraffe tall</u> _____?

2. elephants / can't fly _____?

3. a bird / make a nest _____?

4. kangaroos / have pouch _____?

4 Write. Answer the questions from Activity 3.

1. <u>Because it eats leaves from tall trees</u> _____.

2. _____.

3. _____.

4. _____.

5 Write. Think of a famous person to interview, such as a singer. Write four questions with *why*. Then write the answers.

<u>Why do you sing in English? Because I'm from Canada.</u> _____

_____

_____

_____

_____

_____

_____

Infinitive of purpose

Parrots			wings	**to fly**.	
Cats	use	their	tongues	**to clean**	their fur.
Kangaroos			pouches	**to carry**	their babies.

To + verb describes how or why we do something to reach a goal.

1 **Read.** Circle *to* or *because*.

1. Why do frogs use their back legs?

   Frogs use their back legs **because** / **to** jump.

2. Why does an owl have big eyes?

   Because / **To** it needs to see at night.

3. Why do tigers have sharp teeth?

   Because / **To** they need them to eat meat.

4. Why do penguins have wings?

   Penguins have wings **because** / **to** swim in the sea.

5. Why do kangaroos have pouches?

   Kangaroos have pouches **because** / **to** carry their babies inside.

2 **Read and write.** Use words from the box.

catch   ~~clean~~   drink   fly   run   stay

1. Giraffes use their tongues _____to clean_____ their ears.

2. Bears use their fur _____ warm.

3. Lions use their sharp claws _____ other animals.

4. Elephants use their trunks _____ water.

5. Ostriches use their long legs _____ fast.

6. Parrots use their wings _____.

22

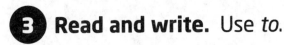 **Read and write.** Use *to*.

1. What do you use to carry your books?

   I use a backpack to carry my books   .

2. What do you use to brush your teeth?

   _____.

3. What do you use to talk to friends?

   _____.

4. Why do you study and do your homework?

   _____.

 Write. Write sentences with *to*.

1. frogs / long tongue

   Frogs use their long tongues to catch flies   .

2. butterflies / wings

   _____.

3. monkeys / hands

   _____.

4. owls / big eyes

   _____.

 Write. Write four sentences about your body.

   I use my nose to smell flowers.

   _____

   _____

   _____

Unit 6

some and any

Question				Answer					
Are	there	**any**	eggs?	Yes,	there	are	**some**	on the table.	*aren't = are not*
			apples?	No,	there	aren't	**(any)**.		
Is	there	**any**	cheese?	Yes,	there	is	**some**	in the fridge.	*isn't = is not*
			rice?	No,	there	isn't	**(any)**.		

Use *some* and *any* to talk about general amounts.

---

1 **Look and match.** Draw a line.

1. Is there any cheese?

2. Are there any olives?

3. Are there any cookies?

4. Is there any sugar?

a. Yes, there are some.

b. Yes, there is some.

c. No, there isn't any.

d. No, there aren't any.

2 **Read.** Write *some* or *any*.

1. Is there _____*any*_____ orange juice? Yes, there is _____*some*_____ .

2. Is there _____ cake? No, there isn't _____ .

3. Are there _____ cans of soda? Yes, there are _____ .

4. Is there _____ milk? No, there isn't _____ .

5. Are there _____ bananas? Yes, there are _____ .

6. Are there _____ tomatoes? No, there aren't _____ .

3 **Write.** Complete the questions and answers.

1. __Are there any__ bananas?

Yes, __there are some__.

2. _____ slices of bread?

No, _____.

3. _____ oil for cooking?

Yes, _____.

4. _____ strawberry yogurt in the refrigerator?

No, _____.

4 **Look and write questions.** Look in your kitchen for answers.

1. Are there any olives? _____

No, there aren't any olives in my kitchen. _____

2. _____

_____

3. _____

_____

4. RICE _____

_____

5. _____

_____

a few and *a little*

Question				Answer					
Are	there	any	nuts?	Yes,	there	are	**a few**	on the table.	aren't = are not
			olives?	No,	there	aren't	(any).		
Is	there	any	juice?	Yes,	there	is	**a little**	in the bottle.	isn't = is not
			tea?	No,	there	isn't	(any).		

Use *a few* and *a little* to talk about general amounts.

 Read. Cross out foods that don't belong.

A few	A little
tomatoes	milk
~~tea~~	~~sandwiches~~
oil	grapes
soup	sugar
nuts	cans of soda
cereal	bread
noodles	pizza

 Read. Circle the correct answer.

1. Are there any olives? Yes, there are **a little** / **a few**.

2. Is there any rice? Yes, there's **a little** / **a few** in the bag.

3. Is there any apple juice? Yes, there is **a little** / **a few** in the fridge.

4. Are there any cookies? Yes, there are **a little** / **a few**.

5. Is there any sugar? Yes, there's **a little** / **a few** in the sugar bowl.

6. Are there any potatoes? Yes, there are **a little** / **a few** in the bag.

3 **Look at the picnic.** Complete the conversations.

1. <u>Are there any</u> _____ olives?

   <u>Yes, there are a few.</u> _____

2. _____ cake?

   _____

3. _____ bananas?

   _____

4. _____ ice cream?

   _____

5. _____ milk?

   _____

6. _____ grapes?

   _____

4 **Read.** Complete the sentences.

In my refrigerator, there _____ milk and there _____ orange

juice. There _____ eggs on the top shelf, and there _____

butter, too. There _____ yogurt, and there _____ red

strawberries in a bowl. On the bottom shelf, there _____ tomatoes,

and there _____ grapes. What's in your refrigerator?

5 **Write.** Tell what's in your refrigerator.

_____

_____

Read. Circle the correct word.

1. **What / How** does the chicken taste? It **looks / tastes** delicious.

2. **Why / How** were the snacks? They **are / were** salty.

3. **Why / How** do babies eat soft food? **Because / To** they haven't got any teeth.

4. Is there **any / some** soup? No, there isn't **any / some**.

5. Are there **any / some** olives in the jar? Yes, there are a **few / little**.

6. How **was / were** the ice cream? It **was / is** sweet and delicious!

 Read. Circle the letter.

1. How does the cake look?
   a. It tastes delicious.
   b. It looks beautiful.
   c. Because it's my birthday.
   d. There is a little.

2. How was the music?
   a. I like quiet music.
   b. It sounds loud.
   c. It is quiet.
   d. It was loud.

3. Is there any juice?
   a. Yes, there is a little.
   b. It tastes sweet.
   c. Yes, there are a few.
   d. Because I'm thirsty.

4. Are there any lemons?
   a. Yes, there is a little.
   b. No, there aren't any.
   c. They taste sour.
   d. No, there isn't any.

5. Why do you go to school on Saturday morning?
   a. To get up early.
   b. Because it feels terrible.
   c. Because I have a music class.
   d. Because I go by bus.

3 **Look and write.** Complete the questions and answers.

1. ___Are there any___ lemons? __Yes, there are a few. They taste sour.__

2. _____ cake? _____

3. _____ apples? _____

4. _____ nuts? _____ potato chips.

5. _____ tea? _____ coffee.

6. _____ chili peppers? _____

4 **Look and write.** Write four sentences about the picture. Use the words in the box.

| any |
| because |
| a few |
| a little |
| some |
| to |

__There are a few bees under the hive. Bees have wings to fly.__

_____

_____

_____

29

Unit 7

Simple past: *Yes/No* questions and short answers

Question				Answer						
	you	**brush**	your	teeth?		I		I		*didn't =*
Did	he	**make**	his	bed?	Yes,	he	**did**.	No, he	**didn't**.	*did not*
	they	**do**	their	homework?		they		they		

Use *did* + subject + the base form of the verb to make a *yes/no* question in the simple past.

1 **Look and read.** Circle the letter.

1.

Did you move your legs?
a. Yes, I did.   b. No, I didn't.

Did you sit down?
a. Yes, I did.   b. No, I didn't.

2.

Did he use his muscles?
a. Yes, he did.   b. No, he didn't.

Did he touch his toes?
a. Yes, he did.   b. No, he didn't.

2 **Read.** Complete the questions and answers.

1. _____ Veronica visit her grandma yesterday?

   Yes, _____.

2. _____ you clean your shoes? Yes, _____.

3. _____ Dani and Martin play tennis yesterday?

   No, _____.

4. _____ Marc do his homework? No, _____.

Read and write. Look at the list. Write the questions and answers.

Feed goldfish ✓

Take dog to park ✗

Have a healthy snack ✓

Wash dishes ✗

Stretch muscles ✓

1. ___Did you feed___ the goldfish yesterday?

___Yes, I did___ .

2. _____ the dog to the park?

_____ .

3. _____ a healthy snack?

_____ .

4. _____ the dishes?

_____ .

5. _____ your muscles?

_____ .

4 **Read and write.**

1. Lizzy / take a shower / before breakfast (yes)

___Did Lizzy take a shower before breakfast? Yes, she did.___

2. Hector / eat fruit (no)

_____

3. the children / stretch muscles / before the game (yes)

_____

4. Toni and Lina / watch TV / yesterday (no)

_____

5. the doctor / wash his hands (yes)

_____

too and enough

too much/too many				enough				
I	eat	**too**	**much**	junk food.	I	don't	eat	**enough**	vegetables.
I	work	**too**	**many**	hours.	I		get	**enough**	exercise.

Use *too much*, *too many*, and *enough* before nouns to talk about amounts.

 Read. Circle the letter.

1. I drink ten cans of soda every day. That's _____!
   a. enough   b. too many

2. I watch _____ TV.
   a. too   b. too much

3. She always stays up _____ late.
   a. enough   b. too

4. He plays basketball every day. He _____ exercise.
   a. gets enough   b. doesn't get enough

5. They sleep for only five hours every night. They _____ sleep.
   a. get enough   b. don't get enough

 Read and write. Use *enough* or *too*.

1. He only eats one apple a week. He doesn't eat ____enough____ fruit.

2. It's hot today. Do we have _____ water for everyone?

3. This exercise is _____ difficult!

4. My mom thinks we watch _____ many soccer games on TV.

5. It's important to get _____ exercise.

6. Don't stay up _____ late! You have school in the morning.

7. Don't eat _____ much junk food. It's bad for you!

3 **Complete the poster for a healthy life.** Write *enough, too much,* or *too many.*

Eat _____ fresh fruit.

Don't eat _____ junk food.

Drink _____ water.

Don't drink _____ soda.

Don't watch _____ TV shows.

Do _____ exercise.

4 **Write about you.** Use *enough, too much,* or *too many* in your sentences.

I _____ soda.

I _____ water.

I _____ fruit.

I _____ potato chips.

I _____ TV.

5 **Write.** Your friend wants to get fit. Write sentences to help. Use the words in the box.

| enough   it's (very) important   too many   too much |

It's important to eat enough vegetables._____

_____

_____

_____

Unit 8

Simple past: regular verbs

Question				Answer			
Did	you	watch	the fireworks?	Yes,	we	**watched**	them.
		like	the party?		I	**liked**	it.

add *ed*: *smell → smell**ed***   *listen → listen**ed***
add *d*:   *like → lik**ed***   *dance → danc**ed***

 Read and write.

1. Did you celebrate Mom's birthday? Yes, we ___celebrated___ Mom's birthday.

2. Did your friends play a game? Yes, we all _____ a game.

3. Did you dance to the music? Yes, we _____ to the music.

4. Did you like the celebration? Yes, I _____ the celebration.

 Read. Write the question.

1. _Did he listen to music_ _____?
   Yes, he listened to music.

2. _____?
   Yes, we watched the fireworks.

3. _____?
   Yes, my sister dressed up in a tiger costume.

4. _____? Yes, we played hide-and-seek.

5. _____? Yes, I painted my face like a lion.

6. _____? Yes, my mom cooked a lot of food.

3 **Read and write.** Use the words from the box.

~~celebrate~~   cook   dance   dress up   paint   taste   walk   watch

Yesterday, my family ___celebrated___ Chinese New Year. We _____

everything red! It's a lucky color. My family _____ a lot of

special food for our friends. It _____ delicious. In the afternoon,

we _____ the dragon parade. We _____ in costumes

and masks. Lots of people _____ in the parade, and some people

_____ to the music. It was full of color and a lot of fun!

4 **Reread Activity 3.** Write the questions and answers.

1. celebrate / Chinese New Year   ___Did they celebrate Chinese New Year?___

   ___Yes, they celebrated Chinese New Year.___

2. cook / special food   _____

   _____

3. watch / parade   _____

   _____

4. dress up / in costumes   _____

   _____

5 **Write.** Write about a celebration. Use the words in the box.

celebrate   dress up   like   listen to   taste   watch

_____

_____

_____

Simple past: irregular verbs

Question				Answer			
Did	you	wear	a mask?	Yes,	I	**wore**	one.
		buy	her a present?			**bought**	her one.

make → made   have → had

1 **Write.** Change the verbs so they tell about the past.

eat _____ate_____   ride _____

drink _____   see _____

give _____   sing _____

go _____   take _____

have _____   wear _____

make _____   write _____

2 **Read.** Write the question.

1. _Did she write the invitations_ _____?
Yes, she wrote the invitations.

2. _____?
Yes, my class had a party.

3. _____?
Yes, my cousins came to the party.

4. _____?
Yes, we swam in the pool.

5. _____?
Yes, my brother rode his bike in the parade.

6. _____?
Yes, I took some balloons.

3 **Read and write.** Complete the questions and answers.

1. _____Did_____ you drink juice?

Yes, I _____drank_____ juice.

2. _____ you eat cake?

Yes, we _____ cake.

3. _____ the children wear masks?

Yes, they _____ masks.

4. _____ your dad take photos?

Yes, he _____ a lot of photos.

5. _____ your best friend buy you a present?

Yes, she _____ me a present.

6. _____ you write a thank-you card?

Yes, I _____ a thank-you card.

4 **Read and write.** Use the words in parentheses.

The children really _____had_____ (have) fun at the party yesterday.

They _____ (wear) party hats and _____ (sing)

the birthday song. They also _____ (swim) in the pool and

_____ (make) decorations. They _____ (eat) chocolate

cake and _____ (drink) lemonade. At the end of the party, all the

children _____ (be) very tired!

5 **Write.** Write about a party you went to. Use the words in the box.

| drink   eat   ~~go~~   have   make   see   sing   take   wear |

I went to my friend's birthday party last weekend.

_____

_____

_____

Unit 9

Simple past: *wh-* questions and negative

Question	Answer				
How was your weekend?	It was boring. I	**didn't**	**have** fun.		*didn't = did not*
What did you do last weekend?	I	**didn't**	**go out**.	I stayed home.	
What did your brother do?	He	**didn't**	**stay** home.	He played in a soccer game.	
Did his team win?	No,	they	**didn't**	**win**.	They lost.

Use *didn't* + the base form of the verb.

 Read. Complete the chart.

Yes	No
I ate a pizza.	I _____ a pizza.
I went to the movies.	I _____ to the movies.
I _____ TV.	I didn't watch TV.
My team won.	My team _____.

 Read and write.

1. Did you play basketball this weekend?

   No, I _____ basketball.

2. Did you visit the museum?

   No, I _____ the museum.

3. Did you see your friends?

   No, I _____ my friends. I texted them.

4. Did you go to the beach?

   No, I _____ to the beach. I went to the park.

Unscramble the questions. Then answer them.

1. weekend / do / did / this / you / what
   <u>What did you do this weekend? I went to the museum.</u>

2. weekend / was / your / how
   _____

3. you / stay / did / home
   _____

4. you / do / what / did
   _____

5. did / do / friends / what / your
   _____

4 **Read about Noah's weekend.** Complete the conversation.

	Saturday	Sunday
Morning	Visit science museum	Stay home
Afternoon	Watch soccer game on TV	Have picnic in the park
Evening	Eat dinner with friends	Go to movies

EZRA: How _____ weekend?

NOAH: It was great. I _____ on Saturday morning.

EZRA: _____ on Sunday morning?

NOAH: I _____.

EZRA: _____ shopping on Saturday afternoon?

NOAH: No, I _____ shopping. I _____ on TV.

EZRA: _____ home on Saturday evening?

NOAH: No, I _____ home. I _____ with my friends.

EZRA: _____ video games on Sunday evening?

NOAH: No, I _____ video games. I _____. I saw _Lost Worlds_. It was cool!

go + verb + -ing

Question					Answer		
What	do	you	do	on the weekend?	I	**go**	**swimming**.
	did					**went**	**hiking**.
					I	**didn't go**	**shopping**.
What	does	she	do	on the weekend?	She	**goes**	**swimming**.
	did					**went**	**hiking**.
					She	**didn't go**	**shopping**.

Use *go* + verb + *-ing* to talk about activities you do in your free time.

1 **Read.** Circle the correct answer.

1. I usually go hiking, but last weekend, I didn't **go** / **went** hiking.

2. My mother **usually** / **went** goes swimming, but last night, she didn't **go swimming** / **swam**.

3. They usually **go** / **went** skateboarding in the park. Yesterday, they went **rode bikes** / **bike riding**.

2 **Read and write.** Use the words in parentheses.

1. We usually ___go walking___ in the park. Last weekend, we _didn't go walking_ in the park. We ___went hiking___ in the forest. (go walking / go hiking)

2. Naomi usually _____ by the river. Last weekend, she _____. She _____. (go running / go horseback riding)

3. The children usually _____ on Saturdays. Last Saturday, they _____. They _____ in the mountains. (go swimming / go skiing)

4. My grandmother usually _____ on weekends. Last weekend, she _____. She _____ with my grandfather. (go shopping / go fishing)

3 **Look and write.** Unscramble the questions. Then answer them.

1.

you / do / on / what / do / weekends

<u>What do you do on weekends?</u>

<u>I usually go hiking.</u>

2.

last / what / weekend / did / do / Inma

_____

_____

3.

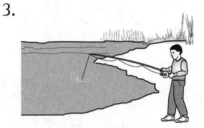

does / Carlos / weekends / do / what / on

_____

_____

4.

last / what / did / Myra / weekend / do

_____

_____

4 **Write.** Answer the questions about your weekend.

What do you usually do on weekends?

_____

What did you do last weekend?

_____

Review: Units 7–9

1 Read. Circle the letter.

1. Michelle is eight, not seven. You didn't buy _____ birthday candles.
   a. too   b. enough   c. too much

2. How _____ your weekend?
   a. did   b. wasn't   c. was

3. What _____ she usually do on weekends?
   a. did   b. does   c. didn't

4. Don't eat _____ chocolate before dinner!
   a. too much   b. usually   c. enough

5. Did your team win? No, we _____.
   a. lose   b. didn't   c. won

6. We didn't eat at a restaurant last night. We _____ at home.
   a. ate   b. eat   c. too much

2 Read and write. Use the words in parentheses.

1. They usually _____ (wear) a uniform to school. Yesterday they
   _____ (wear) jeans.

2. Last weekend, I _____ (not go) horseback riding.
   I _____ (ride) my bike.

3. He usually _____ (watch) soccer on TV. Last night, he
   _____ (go) to the stadium.

4. Last weekend, my mom _____ (buy) me a costume for the
   parade, but she _____ (not buy) me a mask.

5. We _____ (see) Sade in the park last Sunday. We _____
   (not usually see) her on Sundays.

3 Look and write. Complete the questions and answers.

1. How _____ (be) your weekend?

   It _____

2. What _____ (eat) at the party?

   They _____

3. What _____ (wear) in the parade?

   The children _____

4. _____ (see) fireworks?

   No, I _____

5. _____ (eat) a feast?

   Yes, we _____

4 Write. You're talking with your best friend about last weekend. Write the conversation using words from the box.

did   didn't   enough   how   too (much/many)

_____

_____

_____

_____

Review: Units 1–9

 1 Read. Circle the letter.

1. When does she brush her teeth?
   a. After breakfast.   b. To clean them.
2. Why do people dress up?
   a. Before they go out.   b. Because it's fun.
3. Are there any balloons in the sky?
   a. Yes, there are a few.   b. There were enough.
4. Did your dad take the subway?
   a. No, he didn't.   b. He usually takes the bus.
5. How was your weekend?
   a. Saturday and Sunday.   b. It was great!
6. What do you do before you go to bed?
   a. I always go to bed.   b. I usually read a book.

2 Read. Circle the correct answer.

This food **feels / looks / sounds** delicious! I think there is **too many / any / enough** food in the refrigerator for a picnic. There isn't **too many / sometimes / any** junk food. Dad bought **some / any / a few** cheese **but / because / to** make sandwiches. And Mom **get / did get / got** some apples, too. We only need **a little / too much / a few** water. This will be a great picnic!

 3 Read. Complete the sentences with a form of *do*.

1. A crocodile eats meat and a tiger _____, too.

2. What _____ you usually _____ on weekends?

3. We _____ see the parade yesterday because it was raining.

4. What _____ your friend _____ last weekend?

4 **Read and write.** Use the words in the box.

any	can	do	a few	how
next to	right	straight	where	

Tom: Excuse me, _____ you help me?

Mr. Soto: Sure. _____ can I help?

Tom: _____ is Grove Park?

Mr. Soto: You need to turn _____ at the church. Then you go
          _____. It's _____ the river. Or, you can take
          the ferry to the park.

Tom: OK, thanks. Are there _____ museums near the park?

Mr. Soto: Yes, there are _____ museums. I like going to museums.

Tom: I _____, too!

5 **Look and write.** Tell how Paola goes to school. Use *always*,
usually, *sometimes*, or *never* and the word in parentheses.

	M	T	W	T	F
bus	✓				
car					
walk with friends		✓	✓	✓	✓
walk with brother		✓	✓		

1. Paola _____ (take) the bus to school.

2. She _____ (go) by car.

3. She _____ (walks) to school with her friends.

4. Paola's brother _____ (walk) to school with her and her friends.

6 **Write.** Ask questions with *why*. Then write answers with *because* or *to*.

1. touch toes <u>Why did you touch your toes? To stretch my muscles. / Because I</u> <u>wanted to stretch my muscles.</u>

2. exercise _____

_____

3. go to the museum _____

_____

4. go to bed on time _____

_____

7 **Read.** Write questions.

1. _____ This music sounds beautiful.

2. _____ It's between the supermarket and the bakery.

3. _____ Yes, there are a few.

4. _____ To help them fly.

5. _____ It was really boring!

8 **Write.** Write about a concert or celebration that you attended recently. Say where it was and why you went.

_____

_____

_____

_____

GAME

Unscramble the words. Use the words to complete the sentences. Cross each word out after you use it. Write two sentences with the word you don't cross out.

ssnudo	idd	ighsrtat
_____	_____	_____
ogenuh	rwee	roebfe
_____	_____	_____
humc	yhw	efw
_____	_____	_____
nya	tbu	ellitt
_____	_____	_____

1. _____ do kangaroos have pouches?

2. Go _____ on Bellvue Street, and then turn left.

3. Are there _____ potato chips?

4. The children are laughing. The party _____ fun!

5. There is a _____ soup if you are hungry.

6. Let's go swimming _____ we go to bed.

7. I have a _____ masks. You can choose one to wear.

8. How _____ the fireworks? They were loud!

9. I ate too _____ cake. Now I feel sick.

10. We didn't have _____ people to play the game.

11. _____ they take photos of the parade yesterday? No, they didn't.

The word not crossed out is: _____

1. _____

2. _____

47